THE FINAL LETTERS TO
LATIN NORTH AFRICA

Pope Leo IX
Bishop of Rome

Translated by: D.P. Curtin

THE FINAL LETTER TO LATIN NORTH AFRICA

Copyright @ 2024 Dalcassian Press LLC

All rights reserved. No part of this publication may be reproduced, distributed, or transmitted in any form or by any means, including photocopying, recording, or other electronic or mechanical methods, without the prior written permission of the publisher, except in the case of brief quotations embodied in critical reviews and certain other non-commercial uses permitted by copyright law. For permission request, write to Dalcassian Press LLC at dalcassianpublishing at gmail.com

ISBN: 979-8-8693-6156-1 (Paperback)

Library of Congress Control Number:
Author: Curtin, D.P. (1985-)

Printed by Ingram Content Group, 1 Ingram Blvd, La Vergne, Tennessee

First printing edition 2024.

THE FINAL LETTER TO LATIN NORTH AFRICA

THE FINAL LETTER TO LATIN NORTH AFRICA

LETTER TO THOMAS, ARCHBISHOP OF CARTHAGE

Epistle of St. Leo IX to Thomas the African bishop. He pointed out that the Carthaginian archbishop was the leader of all Africa. The bishop of Gummitan was ordered to consecrate the bishops by consent, nor to sit in the provincial council; to depose the Roman pontificate and to depose the bishops and to appoint general councils.

IN THE YEAR 1053

Bishop Leo, servant of God's servants, to Thomas, his beloved brother and co-bishop.

When we recall, on the authority of the venerable canons, that two hundred and five bishops were present at the Carthaginian council, and when we hear from your fraternity that scarcely five bishops survived in all of Africa, certainly in the third part of this corruptible world, we sympathize with all the entrails of our soul at your great loss. But when we learn that the very remains of Christianity were taught to be dispersed by mutual and mutual dissension, and

THE FINAL LETTER TO LATIN NORTH AFRICA

to be inflamed against each other by zeal and contention, another thing first occurred to us to say, like that of the most holy Amos: Spare me, Lord, spare me, I beseech you: who will raise up Jacob, because he is a parent? (Am. 7) But although we are very sorry for such and such a lack of religion; We rejoice greatly, however, because you demand the sixty-seventh of your mother, the holy Roman Church, and expound upon your questions; religious beginning You know, therefore, without a doubt that, after the Roman pontiff, the first archbishop and greatest metropolitan of all Africa is the bishop of Carthage, and that, whoever he may be, that Bishop of Gummuitan has no license to consecrate bishops, or to depose, or to convene a provincial council of Babel, without the consent of the archbishop of Carthage, whose dignity or power let it be, with the exception of those which belong to the proper parish; Forever, he will act with the advice of the Carthaginian archbishop, just as he did with the African bishop there. Our fellow-bishops Peter and John of Undecharissin feel correctly about the dignity of the Carthaginian Church, and they do not agree with the error of the Gummitan Church. I do not want this to be hidden from you before, that it should not be left aside from the decision of the Roman Pontiff that a universal council should be held, or that bishops should be condemned and deposed; but you are permitted to examine certain bishops, and you are not permitted to give a definitive opinion without consulting the Roman Pontiff, as has been said: which, if you seek, you can find in the holy canons. For although it was said by the Lord to all the apostles in general: Whatever shall be bound on earth shall be bound in heaven (Matt. 18), yet it was not without reason that Blessed Peter, the chief of the apostles, was said to Peter the chief of the apostles: You are Peter, and on this rock I will build my church : and I will owe you the keys of the ruler of the heavens (Matt. 16). And in another place: Strengthen your brothers (Luke 22). Of course, because the greatest and most difficult cases of all the churches are to be defined by the saint and principal B. Peter, his successors. Now that we have decided to answer the questions also of our brother bishops Peter and John; we pray that your holy fraternity will not constantly watch over the mutilations of the holy Catholic Church, and devoutly pray for us, always preserve the holy and individual Trinity, most dear brother.

Given on the 16th day of January, in the fifth year of Leo IX, of the seventh indictment.

LETTER TO PETER & JOHN, PRIESTS OF THE AFRICAN CHURCH

St. Leo IX praises the bishops Peter and John for having held a council on ecclesiastical matters at their command and for defending the rights of the archbishop of Carthage against the bishop of Gummitan.

IN THE YEAR 1053

Bishop Leo, servant of the servants of God, greetings and apostolic blessing to the beloved brothers in Christ, the bishops Peter and John.

We lament the fact that the African Churches are so congregated with agents that only barely five bishops can be found, where once two hundred and five were used to be counted by plenary councils; and there the Lord's innumerable flock of many sheep, under numerous rams, rejoiced in high peace. But imputing these things to our sins, lets us fear the justice of the Creator, and earnestly ask for his mercy, that he may at last deign to look upon our servants. But what you wrote to us, thanking the Lord for the state of the holy Roman Church and our safety, you begged: you will know that we thank your fraternity, and always pray for your consolation. And truly, brethren, this is acceptable to our Lord Jesus Christ, that he should look upon and visit the head of all wonders; but the members seek and desire without ceasing the safety of their head. You have indeed done well in that you have held a council on ecclesiastical affairs, which we ordered you to do every year or once. Moreover, you rightly defended the dignity of the Carthaginian church against the Gummitan bishop; because without a doubt the first archbishop after the Roman pontiff and the whole of Africa can lose the privilege once suspected by the holy Roman and apostolic see: but he will maintain it until the end of the age, and until the name of our Lord Jesus Christ is invoked in it, whether Carthage lies desolate or rises glorious sometimes. This is clearly shown from the council of the blessed martyr Cyprian, this from the synod of Aurelius, this from all the African councils, this, which is greater, from the painstaking decrees of our venerable predecessors, the Romans, is clearly shown. Archbishop of Carthage, of whatever rank or power he may be. The Gummitan bishop will only take care of what belongs to his own parish; and the rest, like the other African bishops, will act by the advice of the Archbishop of Carthage, who alone in Africa usually has the mantle from the apostolic see. Under and bishops retain the principal and ancient right of consecration, as it cannot be understood from the words of Aurelius in the Council of Carthage (Council. Carth. III) chapter thirty, when he says: In the church, to which your sanctities have been deigned to assemble, I believe and almost throughout the diam Dominica we have to order bishops, etc. But do not let this be hidden from you, do not deny the opinion of the Roman pontiff to be held apart from knowledge, or to be condemned or deposed by the bishops; it is not allowed to give Which, if you seek, you can find established in the holy councils: namely, because the greater and more difficult causes of all the Churches, through the holy and principal of the blessed Peter, are to be diffused from his successors, since it is to whom it is divinely given: Strengthen your brothers (Luke 22); and: I will give you the keys of the kingdom of heaven (Matt. 16), etc.

Now, since you require our opinion about the archbishops and metropolitans, the statements of our venerable fathers clearly show it, that is: Clement, Anacletus, Anicetus, and others, where it is also read: they were collated, and they did not teach the apostles. But the order of bishops is one, although some are pitied by others, either because they retain the first states and more named, according to the power or laws of the age, or because they can obtain some privilege of dignity from the holy Fathers for some events of sanctity. For, just as every worldly power is distant from one another in these degrees of dignity, that is to say, Augustus or the emperor is the first, then the Caesars, then kings, leaders and counts and judges; so also, the ecclesiastical dignity ordained by the holy Fathers is found, saying blessed Clement (*Epistle. 1, tom. 1., p. 91*): In these states, in which once great men were their priests and the first teachers of the law, primates or patriarchs were placed, who would justly avoid the rest of the judgments and the greater affairs, who also died not of one province, but of many. Where the heathen archbishops go, Christian archbishops are appointed to preside over each province. But where there was a metropolis, which is interpreted as a mother city, there were metropolitans: they would preside over some province of the greater and matriarchal states from three or four states.

These are sometimes only remembered as metropolitans, and sometimes as archbishops, if there were no greater ones in the province. But where the smaller states had only priests or counts, they were appointed bishops. Moreover, the tribunes of the people do not mean deaf priests, or priests of the lower order of the clergy. The Roman Pontiff was preferred to all these by divine and human privilege. The primates of Africa must be understood differently, because anciently primates were established in each of its provinces, not according to the power of any state, but according to the time of their ordination. but one presides over all of them, that is, the Archbishop of Carthage, who also may not incongruously be called a metropolitan, to prophesy Carthage as the metropolis of all Africa, of which we have mentioned above. Thus, it is read in the Council of Carthage: "The bishop of the first see shall not be called chief priest, or high priest, or anything of the sort, but only the bishop of the first see." Constantly watching over your holy brotherhood with the armies of God's holy Church and praying devoutly for us, may the holy and individual Trinity always preserve it, dearest brothers.

THE FINAL LETTER TO LATIN NORTH AFRICA

LATIN TEXT

THE FINAL LETTER TO LATIN NORTH AFRICA

THE FINAL LETTER TO LATIN NORTH AFRICA

S. Leonis IX epistola ad Thomam episcopum Africanu. Osterdit Carthaginensem archiepiscopum totius Africaeesseprimatem; Gummitanum rero episcopum sineillius consensu nec episcopos consecrare,nec provinciale concilium concocare sesse; soliudautem Romanu pontificisesse et episcopos deponere et generalia concilia indicere.

ANNO 1053

Leo episcopus, servus servorum Dei, Thomae confratri charissimo et coepiscopo, saltum.

Cum ex venerabilium canonum auctoritate recolimus ducentos quinque episcopos concilio interfuisse Carthaginens, et nunca tua fraternitate audimus quinque vix episcopos superessein totaAfrica,utique tertie hujus corruptibilis mundi parte,compatimur tantae vestrae imminutioni totis visceribus animi. Cum autem ipsas Christianitatis reliquias ediscimus interua et mutua dissensione discinai etdispergi,et adversus se invicem zelo et contentione priacipatus inflari, nit aliud nobis primo dicendum occurritquamilludsanti Amos vatis: Parce, Domine, parce, obsecro: quis suscitubit Jacob,quia parentus est? (AmosVII) Sed quamvis in tali tantoque defectu religion is plurimum doleamus; multum tamen gaudemus, quia sanctae Romanae Ecclesiae matris vestrae sextentiam requiritis et exspeciatis super quaestionibus vestris: et quasi rivulis ab uno fonte erumpentibus, et in suo se cursu per diversaspargentibusadipsius fontius primam scaturiginem reverti debere optimum putatis, utinde resumatis directionis vestigiam,unde sumpsistis totius Christianae religiouis exordium. Noveris ergo procul dubio quia, post Romanum pontificent, primus archepiscopuset totius Africae maimus metropolitanus est Carthaginensis episcopus, nec, quicumque sit, ille Gummuitanus episcopus aliquam licentiamconsecradi episcopos, vel deponendi, seu provinciale concilium convocandi babel, sine consensu Carthaginensis archiepiscopi, cujuslibel dignitatis aut potestatis sit, exceptis his quaead propriam parochiam pertinent; aetera autum, sicut et alli Africani episcopi, consilio Carthaginensus archepiscopi aget. Undecharissini canfratres nostri coepiscopi Petrus et Joannes recte sentiunt de Carthaginesis Ecclesia edignitate, nec consentiunt errori Gummitanae Ecclesiae. Hoc antem nolo vos lateat, non dehere praeter sententiau Romanu pontificis universale concilium celebrari, aut episcopos damnari veldeponi; qui etso licetvobis aliquos episcopos examinare, diffinitivam aumen sententiam, absque consultu Romanu pontificis, ut dictum est, non licet dare: quod in sanctis canonibus statitem, si quaeritis, Potestis invenire. Quamvis enim omnibus generaliter apostolis dictum sit a Domino: Quaecumque ligaveridisin terra, ligata erunt et in coelo (Matth. XVIII): tamennon sine causa specialiter et cominatim dictim est B. Petro apostolorum principi: Tu es Petrus, et super hanc petram aedificabo Ecclesiam meam: et tibi debo claves regui coelorum (Matth. XVI). Et in alio loco: Confirma fratres tuos (Luc. XXII) . Scilicet quia omnium Esslesiarum majores et difficilores causae, per sanctum et principalem B. Petri sedema successoribus ejus sunt diffiniendae. Jam quia ad interregata etiam confratrum nostrorum Petri et Joannis episcoporum decrevimus respondere; optamus ne sanctamtuam frateraitatem jugiter invigilantemutilitatibus sanctae catholicae Ecclesiae, atque devote pro nobis orantem, sancta et individua Trinitas semper conserver, charissime frater.

Datum XVI Kalendas Januarii, Anno Domini Leonis papae IX quinto, indictione VII.

THE FINAL LETTER TO LATIN NORTH AFRICA

S. Leo IX Petrum et Joannem episcopos laudat quod jusso suo concilium de rubus ecclesiasticis celebraverint et jura archepiscopi Carthaginensis contra Gummitanum episcopum defenderint.

ANNO 1053

Leo episcopus, servus servorum Dei, dilectissintis in Christo fratribus Patro et Joanni episcopis salutem et apostolicam benedictionem.

Decus Ecclesiarum Africanarum ita conculeatum agentibusnimium dolemus ut modo vix quinque inveniantur episcopi, ubi olimducenti quinque solebant perconcilia plenaria computari; et ibi pauculas oves quotiitianae innumerabilis grex Domini sub numerosis arietibus exsultabat alta pace. Sed haec peccatis nostris imputantes, justitiam Creatoris collandantes, timeanmus, et misericordiam ejus instanter postulemus ut servos snos tandem respicere dignetur. Quod autem scripsistis nobis pro sanctae Romanae Ecclesiae statu nostraque incolumitate vos Dominum gratias agendo exorasse: noveritis nos vestrae fraternitati gratias agere, et pro consolatione vestra semper orare. Et revera, fratres, hoc acceptabile est Domino nostro Jesu Christo ut caput omnibus merabris prospiciat et invisilet; membra vero sui capitis salutem sine intermissione quarant et optent. Bene equidem fecistis, quod jussi a nobis concilium de rebus ecclesiasticis habuistisL quod etiam omni anno vel semel agere debetis. Insuper recte contra Gummitanum episcopum dignitatm Carthaginensis Eccesiae defendistis; quia sine dubio post Romanum pontificem primus archepiscopus et tota Africa potest perdere privelgium semel suspectum a sancta Romana et apostolica sede: sed obtinebit illud usque in finem saeculi, et donec in ea invocabitur nomen Domini nostri Jesu Christi, sive deserta jaceat Carthago, sive resurgat gloriosa aliquando. Hoc ex concilio beati martyris Cypriani, hoc ex synodis Aurelii, hoc ex omnibus Africanis concilis, hoc, quod majus est, ex venerabilium praedecessorum nostrum Romanorum paesulum decretis aperte monstratur: nec quicunque ille sit Gummitanus episcopos vel deponendi, seu provinciale concilium convocandi habet sine consensu Carthaginensis archiepiscopi, cujuslibet dignitatis aut potestatis sit. Tantummodo procurabit ille Gummitanus episcopus que ad propriam parochiam pertinent; caetera autem, sicut et alii episcopi Africani, consilio Carthaginensis archiepiscopi aget, qui solus in Africa pallium ab apostolica sede habere solet. Under et episcopis consecrandi principale et antiquum jus retinet, sicut ex verbis Aurelii in concilio Carthaginensi (Concil. Cartha. III) capitulo trigesimo non potest intelligi, cum dicit: In ecclesia, ad quam dignata est vestr sancitias convenire, credbro ac pene per diam Dominicam episcopis ordinandos habemus, etc. Sed hoc vos non lateat, non dehere praeter scientiam sententiam Romani pontificis universale concilium celebrari, aut episcopis damnari vel deponi, quia, etsi licet vobis aliquod episcopos examinare, diffinitivam tamen sententiam absque consultu Romani pontificis, ut dictum sententiam absque consultu Romani pontificis, ut dictum est, non licet dare. Quod in sanctis caronibus statutem, si quaeritis, potestis invenire: scilicet quia omnium Ecclesiarum majores et difficiliores causae, per sanctam et principalem beati Petri sedm a successoribus ejus diffuiendae sunt, utpote cui divinitus di itur: Confirma frates tuos (Luc. XXII); et: Tibi dabo claves regni caelorum (Matt. XVI), etc.

Nunc, quia de archiepiscopis et metropolitanis sententiam nostram requiritis, venerabilium autecessorum nostrorum dictis aperte demonstrant, id est Clementis, Anacleti, Aniceti et aliorum, ubi item legitur: Sacerdotum ordo bipartitus est, nec amplius quam duos ordines, id est episcoporum et presbyterorum, nobis collati sunt, nec ap stoli docuerunt. EPiscoporum autem ordo unus est, quamvis alii paeferantur aliis, sive pro eo quod primas civitates et magis nominatas, secundum potentiam aut leges saeculi retinent, sive quod a santcis Patribus pro aliqua everentia sanctitatis aliquod privilegium dignitatis possitent. Nam, sicutomnis mundana potestas his gradibus dignitatum a se invicem distat, id est, ut primus sit Augustus vel imperator, deinde Caesares, deinde reges, duces et comites atque trobuni; ita et ecclesiastica dignitas ordinata a sanctis Patribus invenitur, dicente beato Clemente (Epistl. 1, tom 1., p. 91): In his civitatibus, in quibus olim ap dehuios pimi flamines eorum atque primi legis doctores erant, primates vel patriarchae positi sunt, qui reliquorem judicia et majora negotia juste diffuirent, qui etiam non uni provinciae, sed plurilaeus paecessant. Dinle ubi archiflamines eoant paganerum, archiepiscopi instituti sunt Christianorum qui singulis provinciis praessent. Ubi vero metropolis erat, quae interpretatus mater civitas, metropolita inerant: que de tribusaut quat or civitatibus itra aliquam provinciam majori et matriairum civitatum praesidebunt. Isti a iquando metropolitani tantum meminantur, aliquando vero archiepiscopi, si in ip a provincia majores non fuerint aliqui. Ubi autem minores civitates habuerint solummodo flamines vel comites, episcope sunt instituti. Porro tribuni plebis non alsurde intelliguntur presbyteri, sive reiqui inferioris ordinis clerici. His omnibus divino et humano privilegio praelatus est pontifex Romanus de Africae primatibus aliter intelligendum est quia in singulis ejus provinciis antiquitus primates instituebantur non secundum potentia nalicujus civitatis, sed secundum tempus suae ordinationis; quibus tamen omnibus praecrat unus, scilicet Carthaginensis archiepiscopus, qui etiam non incongrue dici potest metropolitanus propeter Carthaginem metropolim totius Africae, quorum supra meminimus. Ita legitur in concilio Carthaginensi, capitulo viges mo sexto: Primae sedis episcopus non appelletur princeps sacerdotum, aut summus sacerdos, aut aliquid hujusmodi, sed tantum primae sedis episcops. Sanctam vestram fraternitatem jugiter invigilantem militatibus sanctae Dei Ecclesiae atque devote pro nobis orantem, sancta et individua Trinitas semper conservet, charissimi fratres.

THE FINAL LETTER TO LATIN NORTH AFRICA

The Scriptorium Project is the work of a small group of lay people of various apostolic churches who are interested in the preservation, transmission, and translation of the works of the early and medieval church. Our efforts are to make the works of the church fathers accessible to anyone who might have an interest in Christian antiquities and the theological, philosophical, and moral writings that have become the bedrock of Western Civilization.

To-date, our releases have pulled from the Greek, Nordic, Visigothic, Slavic, Armenian, Syriac, Georgian, Anglo-Saxon, Byzantine, Persian, German, Celtic, Ethiopian, and Coptic traditions of Christianity, and have been pulled from sundry local traditions and languages.

THE FINAL LETTER TO LATIN NORTH AFRICA

Other Catalogue Titles for the Early Punic Church in North Africa:

Seven Rules by Ticonius the Donatist *(July 2006)*
Letters on the Council of Ephesus by Capreolus of Carthage (Aug. 2007)
The Time of the Barbarians by St. Quoddeusvult of Carthage (Feb. 2009)
Two Letters from Byzantine Africa by Licinianus of Carthage (Oct. 2016)
Apology to Gunthamund, King of Vandals by Blossius Aemilius Dracontius (Feb. 2018)
Letter to Pope Theodore by Victor of Carthage (Feb. 2020)
Against Palladius the Arian by Vigilius of Thapsus (Nov. 2023)
Response Against Arians by St. Fulgentius of Ruspe (Jan. 2024)
The Final Letter to Latin North Africa by Pope Leo IX (Mar. 2024)

www.ingramcontent.com/pod-product-compliance
Lightning Source LLC
LaVergne TN
LVHW061044070526
838201LV00073B/5179